Harold's Lonely Day

An Alphabet Sounds Book

First Edition

Welcome!

I hope you enjoy our phonics story. All twenty-six letters of the alphabet are represented with their characters from the Genesis Curriculum First Step book. The characters meet and interact through this fun story.

Remember to read all of the sounds phonetically. When Elizabeth the Elephant says, "Eeee…" It's the short E sound as in egg. When Bobby the Bee says, "B, b, b," it's "buh" not "be."

Bb

Bobby had been working hard all day, buzzing here and there and back again and again. He was starting to get tired. "B, b, b."

Aa

Bobby happened to be flying near Abraham, who was lazing in his swampy water. When Abraham heard Bobby going, "B, b, b," Abraham got scared and screamed, "Aaaaaa!"

Cc

Caleb, snoozing in the sun nearby, was startled awake by the scream. When he scrambled to his feet, a hair ball got caught in his throat. "C, c, c."

Caleb hacked away until his fur ball came out. Wanting to flee from the embarrassment of the grossness he just spit out, Caleb headed for town. It wasn't long before he happened upon a curious site. A circus tent had been pitched just outside of town. He wandered onto the circus grounds.

Dd

Caleb saw Danielle practicing her latest feat, balancing on a ball on one leg. She could already do it with two legs, and who are we kidding, of course, she could already balance on one leg, duh!

Elizabeth was watching Danielle perform her new trick. Danielle called out to her, "What trick do you want me to do next?"

Elizabeth asked, "Could you bounce upside down on the ball on your head?"

Danielle answered, "Duh, of course!"

Then Elizabeth asked, "Could you do a headstand while spinning the ball on your tail?"

Danielle answered, "Duh! Well, which do you want to see next?" Danielle asked again.

Elizabeth couldn't make up her mind. They both sounded funny. She only answered, "Eeee...."

Danielle didn't have the patience to wait any longer for Elizabeth's answer. Besides, she was distracted by a smell. "Do you smell that Elizabeth?" Danielle asked her elephant pal.

"I don't smell anything, but I hear something," Elizabeth answered.

"I smell fish," Danielle said. "What do you hear?"

"Sounds like ffffffff."

Ii

Elsewhere on the circus grounds, Harold the Hippo was sleeping peaceful with his nose just out of the water. Isaac the Iguana started laughing to himself. He tiptoed over to Harold's holding area.

"I, i, i, i!" Isaac beeped at him, imitating an alarm clock. Harold snapped open his humongous mouth.

"What? What is it?" He stood and his mammoth mass rose from the water. He looked around and saw Isaac.

"Oh, it's you, Isaac. I'm going to get you." Harold started after Isaac, who swiftly fled. Harold was soon panting, out of breath, "H, h, h."

He looked around and shouted, "Who wants to spend time with you, anyhow. I'll go find someone less obnoxious to be around."

Harold wandered off toward the children's petting zoo area.

Gg

Harold greeted Greg the Goat. "How are you this fine morning?" Greg didn't respond. Harold lumbered slowly closer and called out again, "Good morning!"

Greg dug in his back hooves and let out a "G, g, g, get out of here!"

Harold was so startled that he started walking backwards, which is difficult when you are a big guy like Harold. He headed straight back home.

Jj

Joanna the Jaguar came dancing by Harold's habitat.

"J, j, j, j, j, j."

"Hi, Joanna!" Harold called. But Joanna was too focused on her dancing to pay attention. She kept dancing right on past, making her own music as usual, "J, j, j, j, j, j,"

Kk

Karen the Kangaroo had heard Harold. She jumped over the fence around her enclosure and hopped on over to Harold.

"I heard you call to Joanna and saw her ignore you!" Karen said indignantly.

"It seems no one wants to be around me today," Harold said sadly.

"That's nonsense," Karen said. But just then she heard something clanking, "K, k, k, k, k." It was the keys of the animal keeper. He was making the rounds. Karen didn't want to get in trouble for being out of her area and hopped off, leaving Harold alone again.

Ll

"Why does no one want to be around me today?" Harold moaned.

Lee the Lion was wandering past and opened his mouth to speak. Harold thought he was going to answer the question, but all he said was "Llllllllee!" because Lee *loves* the sound of his own name.

Harold just groaned.

Nn

Ned the Nuthatch was feeling kind of miserable. He was sitting on a wire above Harold's home. Harold called out to him, "Ned! Ned!"

But Ned's ears were all plugged up from his cold. All Harold heard him respond was "Nnnn...."

Meanwhile, Michael the Monkey was performing his act. One of his favorite parts was to run through the crowd, up and down the stairs and across the seats. It thrilled the audiences. Of course, Michael's favorite part was snatching a meatball from an unsuspecting audience member. For Michael, it was deliciously fun to be part of the circus.

Michael grabbed a meatball and dashed out of the circus tent. The audience loved his antics. Michael stopped to eat his meatball and leaned back against Olivia's tank while he ate.

"Michael, will you take a look at my throat. Do my tonsils look red to you?"

"I'm eating, Olivia. I don't want to look in your mouth."

"Oh, please! I'm just sure I'm going to need my tonsils removed. What do you think? Please take a look. I can't see into my mouth. Please look for me. Aaaahhhhh."

Mm

"I'm going to find a more suitable dining area," Michael said and took off.

Michael stopped in front of where Harold was sitting and moping. Michael took a big bite of his meatball. "Mmmmm."

Harold asked, "What do you have there?"

Michael pointed to his meatball and just said, "Mmmm...."

"Well, what is it?"

Michael the Monkey popped the rest in his mouth and was only heard saying, "Mmmm..."

"You could have at least shared a little," Harold said as he watched Michael stride away.

Pp

The chilly fall air was bothering Paul. "I can see my breath! P, p, p. I miss my home," he said as he flew, trying to keep warm. "I have an idea," he said and swooped toward Harold's habitat.

Paul called down to the hippo, "Harold! Harold!"

Harold looked up.

"Harold, could I please come sit with you. Would you help me keep warm?"

Harold liked that someone wanted to be with him, even if it was only because he wanted something. Harold was happy to help.

"Sure," Harold said and Paul landed on his broad back.

Qq

Bobby was buzzing around the grounds and flew past Paul perched on Harold's hind-quarters. Bobby decided it looked like a good place to rest. Harold grew a bit nervous when Bobby landed on his nose. Harold was trying to not move a muscle when he saw another bee come flying up to talk to Bobby.

"Bobby, come quick," the bee said. "It's Queenie. You've upset her. She's expecting you back."

"Are you sure?" Bobby asked.

"Of course, I'm sure," the other bee responded. "When I left, she was making that noise. You know, "Qu, qu, qu."

"Uh oh. You're right. She's upset. I have to get going."

Rr

With that, Bobby forced himself up and flew off, and this time Harold was glad that someone had left him alone.

Bobby was on his way back to the hive when he noticed something unusual. He knew he shouldn't stop, but he was curious.

He flew just beyond the fence around the circus grounds. And what did he see? It was a rabbit! It was Robert, and he was tugging and pulling at something. "R, r, r."

Now Bobby was even more curious. What was he trying to get? It seemed buried under the fence. "R, r, r."

Ss

Finally, it came loose. It was a carrot. Or was it? The rabbit sniffed it and then hopped off without it. Bobby flew in closer and saw it was just a stuffed carrot toy a child must have dropped long ago.

Bobby felt badly for the rabbit who had worked so hard for nothing. Then suddenly he felt badly for himself. Queenie would not be pleased! Bobby buzzed off in a hurry.

Harold had been happy when Bobby had flown off with his bee buddy, but suddenly Paul had flown off too. Harold had wondered why until he heard, "Ssss." He looked up and knew exactly why Paul the Parrot had flapped away. Sarah the slithering snake was in a nearby tree.

Uu

Harold was soon distracted when Ulysses came galloping through. As usual he was charging full speed ahead without looking where he was going. "Uh." Ulysses rammed the tree that Sarah had been in. I say "had been in" because Ulysses' blow had knocked her out of the tree. Sarah was on the ground and in a bad mood and looked like she wanted to knock someone over, herself! Oh no!

Tt

Sarah spotted Tabitha sleeping in the sun across the way. Ulysses noticed Sarah moving toward her. Ulysses got to Tabitha first and tapped on her shell to wake her. "T,t,t,t,t."

Tabitha poked her head out of her shell. "Why do I hear, t, t, t, t, when I'm trying to sleep?"

The unicorn told her what was happening.   "Tabitha, quick! Sarah is in a bad mood and she's coming this way. You should get out of here." Tabitha thanked Ulysses and moved away as fast as she could.

Victoria was finished with her act. She rides in a toy ambulance that drives around the circus tent, "Vvvvvvvv." The remote-control operator drove her out of the tent leaving the crowd cheering behind her.

Victoria instantly realized that Tabitha was in danger of a snake attack. She took off and reached Tabitha before Sarah did. She guarded her until an animal handler came to the rescue.

Ww

William the Walrus entered the center circus ring after Victora. He missed all the excitement outside, but he was creating excitement inside. The crowd cheered when he started doing his helicopter act. He spun on his head and his tail cut through the air just like a helicopter blade, "W, w, w, w, w."

Xx

Outside, the animal handler caught Sarah and returned her to her tank. The handler would make sure everyone got back to where they belonged, but he was thirsty. He took out a soda can and leaned back on Xavier's tank. "Kssss." Xavier flipped in his tank. Victoria's remote-control driver came over to join him. "Kssss." Xavier flipped again. Tabitha and Victoria cheered for him.

All of the excitement had distracted Harold from feeling alone. He had almost forgotten about the whole thing when a car pulled up dragging a trailer behind. Harold was curious about what was inside. The doors opened and the animal handler led out a hairy yak, who let out a big yawn, "Yyyyyy."

Zz

"Harold," the animal keeper said, "we need a home for Yolanda here for the time being. Since you stay in the water most of the time, you wouldn't mind her staying here with you, right?" Harold smiled a big smile. He wouldn't be alone anymore.

Harold finally had a happy home, but Bobby had lost his. His delay in getting back to the hive had Queenie furious! She sent him right back out of the hive and told him to find a new queen to serve. Bobby didn't know where to go. He headed back toward the animals to look for a new home. He flew as fast as he could, "Zzzzzzzzzzzzzzz." Zoe's ears perked up. She knows she's allergic to bees and took off as fast as she could go.

Zoe went galloping away. She galloped right out of the circus grounds. She kept going until she was forced to stop at the edge of some swampy water. Who was there in the water? Abraham, of course! And what did he say when Zoe came near? "Aaaaaaaa!"

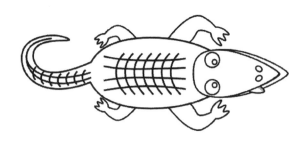

Genesis Curriculum takes a book of the Bible and turns it into daily lessons in science, social studies, and language arts.

GC Steps is a preschool and kindergarten program that prepares children in reading, writing, and math.

GC Math takes learning together an extra measure as children work through Bible-inspired word problems, together and at their own level.

Check out our site for more on our expanding curriculum.

genesiscurriculum.com

Made in the USA
Columbia, SC
09 June 2017